MW00872865

SHAKE
IT UP!

REFRESH AND REDISCOVER YOURSELF THROUGH
WONDER AND BODY-MIND ADVENTURES

AUDREY HAZEKAMP AND
OXANA HOLTMANN

BALBOA.
PRESS
A DIVISION OF HAY HOUSE

Balboa Press books may be ordered through booksellers or by contacting:

Balboa Press
A Division of Hay House
1663 Liberty Drive
Bloomington, IN 47403
www.balboapress.com
1 (877) 407-4847

Because of the dynamic nature of the Internet, any web addresses or links contained in this book may have changed since publication and may no longer be valid. The views expressed in this work are solely those of the author and do not necessarily reflect the views of the publisher, and the publisher hereby disclaims any responsibility for them.

The author of this book does not dispense medical advice or prescribe the use of any technique as a form of treatment for physical, emotional, or medical problems without the advice of a physician, either directly or indirectly. The intent of the author is only to offer information of a general nature to help you in your quest for emotional and spiritual well-being. In the event you use any of the information in this book for yourself, which is your constitutional right, the author and the publisher assume no responsibility for your actions.

Any people depicted in stock imagery provided by Thinkstock are models, and such images are being used for illustrative purposes only.
Certain stock imagery © Thinkstock.

Print information available on the last page.

ISBN: 978-1-5043-5697-8 (sc)
ISBN: 978-1-5043-5699-2 (hc)
ISBN: 978-1-5043-5698-5 (e)

Library of Congress Control Number: 2016906937

Balboa Press rev. date: 07/06/2016

PRAISE FOR SHAKE IT UP!

"The essence of life is activity, change, growth, while death's agenda is stasis, stuckness, stagnation. Shake It Up is a summons to stir your juices, and get the process rolling forward. Changed attitudes lead to changed behaviors which lead to changed consequences. Holtmann and Hazekamp provide thoughtful challenges to our thinking and practices which, if one follows their promptings, leads to a reinvigorated life."
- James Hollis, Ph. D., Jungian analyst and author

"Daily life can pull us away from the soul nurturance that makes life worth living. "Shake it Up!" is the perfect companion for the ongoing journey back in again, to your essential nature, your true self. Rich with activities and invitations, this journal provides the bridge from the contraction of Reactive Brain to the infinite possibilities of the land of Creative Brain. Pick it up and Shake it Up!"
- Julie Colwell, Ph.D., psychologist and author

"This exciting new journal of inspiration and wisdom will open your eyes, deepen your heart, and fill your spirit with wonder. If you're ready to energize your life, and grow in ways you never expected, Shake It Up is for you!"
- Mark Matousek, Author of *When You're Falling, Dive: Lessons in the Art of Living*

"A true come-as-you-are toolkit that will expand your understanding of your beautiful self and your appreciation of your extraordinary life. With simple, thought-provoking questions, this workbook is both a warm hug and a sparkly invitation to your truest, best self."
- Samantha Bennett, The Organized Artist Company

"At some point in our lives, it seems like we stop doing what brings us joy. We stop asking powerful questions and accept the status quo. Thankfully Audrey and Oxana have the perfect remedy to create a positive shift in your personal or professional life with the appropriately named book, 'Shake It Up!'. This book is chock full of nuggets of wisdom, creative activities that offer new perspectives, and most importantly, an all to forgotten reminder to not only appreciate others, but also ourselves."
- Antonio Neves, Leadership speaker, author and award-winning journalist

ACKNOWLEDGEMENTS

I would like to thank my husband, Martin, who keeps encouraging me to write and create. I am grateful to my children, Benjamin, Jonathan, and Alina for being a natural example of how to live in discovery and play without fear. I deeply appreciate my wonderful friend Audrey for her infinite curiosity, innovative mastery, and ability to fill our co-creative process with realness, joy, and celebration.
—Oxana Hotlmann

Big thanks to my global family who get excited with big questions and exploring the possibilities that come with them. I express huge waves of appreciation to my co-creator, Oxana, for her exquisite sense of order and harmony and for continuing to nudge my insatiable hunger for asking the big questions and exploring the unknown.
—Audrey Hazekamp

Both of us are deeply grateful to our mentors, Drs. Gay and Kathlyn Hendricks, whose relationship and creative insights are an endless source of inspiration.

DEDICATION

To all of the courageous explorers of inner and outer terrains,
who are devoted to playing and asking the question,
"Now what's possible?"

FOREWORD

Why would you want to shake things up in your life rather than hunker down and hold on tight through turbulent times? Alan Watts, among other philosophers, eloquently advocated the wisdom of insecurity over fifty years ago, attempting to integrate Eastern spiritual traditions with our Western go-go, do-do pragmatism. More recently, scientists from many disciplines extol the value of "pattern-interrupt" to enliven your physical, emotional and interactive smarts. Shake It Up is the most fun way yet to loosen habits and routines, find delight in discovery and generate wonder reliably. I particularly love the ease and accessibility of the tools that Oxana and Audrey introduce. They're powerfully simple and simply effective—and fun. Who knew learning could be fun?! Wait, we have evidence about that now too. People only learn when they're having a good time. Shake It Up generates such a good time that you may not realize how much you're learning and the ease and flexibility that are becoming part of your daily life until you encounter a previously terrifying dragon and extinguish the flames by welcoming the power of your integrated self.

We know now that learning to let go of old beliefs and patterns that may have first emerged centuries ago enhances creativity, connection and wellbeing. What you'll find in this engaging journal are whole-person activities that use body intelligence principles to accelerate not just learning, not just mindfulness, but embodiment. You'll learn how to feel at home in yourself and to welcome the unknown as a window to wonder. When the wobbles arrive, you'll learn to dance with uncertainty and find your ground easily wherever you are in the moment.

Both Audrey and Oxana live their work and have befriended the inner saboteurs that we all carry. They speak with the confidence of allies and explorers who have brought their gifts back from the wild shores to share with other consciousness enthusiasts. The rhythm of the journal will engage you immediately, structured as it is around core skills that you integrate through practice in different aspects of your life in easy chunks.

There's plenty of data and application to keep your mind interested and plenty of variety and innovation to expand your responsiveness and build your creative muscles. You'll be held in the intimacy of journaling and encouraged to make one choice at a time that takes you into expanded realms inside and around you. I'm excited for the journey you're beginning and wish you ever-expanding joy.

Kathlyn Hendricks, Ph.D., BC-DMT
Master trainer and teacher, Best-selling author of *Conscious Loving and Conscious Loving Ever After*

SIX REASONS YOU'LL LOVE THE SHAKE IT UP! JOURNAL

1. You will remember how to play and reconnect with your innovative self.

Knowing how to play is an evolutionary requirement! Research shows that play keeps our brain and body young and flexible. Adults who choose to play become more lighthearted, compassionate, resilient to change, and optimistic. On the other hand, resisting or denying our natural instinct to play leads to a sense of stagnation and "stuckness." The goal of the journal is to jump-start your playful nature, which will allow you to create a sense of renewal, innovation, and joy in many areas of your life.

2. You will develop an empowering habit of appreciating others and yourself.

Mastering the art of appreciation is a lifelong adventure. This journal provides the perfect nudge for a fresh look at life through the question "What is here to appreciate?" or "What wants attention and love here now?"

Genuine appreciation has been shown scientifically to raise levels of feel-good hormones. Professor John M. Gottman, known for his work in the field of relationships, established that all healthy relationships require at least five expressions of appreciation for every criticism or negative remark. The flow of appreciation, whether in giving or receiving, confirms and strengthens your ability to notice good things in life. It opens the channels for enjoyment and connection with yourself and others.

3. You will free up your sense of wonder and stimulate new perspectives.

This journal is filled with wonder-activating questions. These questions stimulate and grow your internal curiosity and skill for wondering. Wondering trains your system to be open to discovery rather than settling in on a known outcome or needing to have the right answer. Genuine wonder is the space of ingenuity where new possibilities and creative solutions are born through ease. Prominent innovators in the areas of science, business, and communication all share the skill of asking powerful questions. Through pondering these wonder-activating questions and practicing wonder, you will begin to ask your own life-inspiring questions and perhaps stimulate your own innovative problem solving.

4. You will discover effective processes for facilitating change, personally and professionally.

You can use the activities in this journal as a launching pad to create your own explorations and share them with your colleagues and clients for maximal positive collaborations and powerful connections. All of the practices and activities in the journal have been solo and group tested and are effective with both children and adults.

5. You will gain insight into how to create a nourishing environment for your ongoing personal growth and evolution.

Real learning only happens while you are having a good time. Within this journal are pages and pages of activities that invite a foundation of appreciation, discovery, and creative expression — environments that support flourishing in your own life's journey through creative fun. These practices are designed to assist you in creating a sacred and safe space to be in a state of real learning that is effective, efficient, and sustainable.

6. You will gather a collection of your growth explorations to review and repeat.

Many of us who love discovering the world and ourselves don't bother to create aphysical space for collecting our insights and "aha" moments. We found that it's extremely valuable to return to your self-explorations, read through them and add to them, so you can integrate them into your everyday life. The journal provides you with a physical space to create a track record of your own life laboratory experiments and new wonderful discoveries about yourself. All your discoveries are in one accessible place!

HOW IT WORKS

The journal is brimming with enticing activities, wonder questions, and active explorations that inspire you to acknowledge and enjoy your creative inquiry. It stokes the fires of fun, body intelligence, enthusiastic curiosity, and emotional literacy.

You will be offered irresistible invitations to live life one courageous adventure and one full expression at a time. This journal allows you to discover how to best navigate your own evolution YOUR WAY. This means you choose whatever generates energy, provides insight into possibility, and ignites new levels of awareness. The result is that you will remember how to play, increase your vitality, and make curiosity a delightful habit.

There is a variety of activities each week that keep things fresh and interesting. However, no rules dictate that you need to go in order. You might choose to date your explorations and keep track of your discoveries as a source of personal information and appreciation for what you have already completed. The most important part is that you navigate this journal in ways that provide the most fun for you.

WHY SHAKE IT UP?

Researchers say that, on average, we have between sixty thousand and eighty thousand thoughts per day. Amidst all of these seemingly brilliant thoughts, approximately 95 percent are recycled, be it from yesterday or from early childhood. Genuinely creative thoughts and ideas that are followed by new courageous actions are revolutionary, renewing, and refreshing!

Are you ready to shake up your repetitive thoughts and patterns?

Many of us were well trained to generate the result or the answer that is expected from us. "Tell me what I should produce or what I am supposed to experience, and I will do my best to achieve it" is the familiar mind-set. The activities in this journal come free of expectation and invite you to stretch into your creative mind and body intelligence. They invite you to experience the unknown as friendly and worth exploring.

With the intention of having a good time, first let yourself dive into an experience —appreciating from your heart, wondering with an open mind, drawing, getting up from your chair and playing and then record your results, insights, and perspectives. It's impossible to do it wrong.

Fully engaging with each activity clears a path to enjoying life on new levels. It is empowering to know that you are free to come up with your own answers and create results from your own experience. It also dissolves the illusion that many of us share — that one day we will reach a state of static perfection and "arrive"! Each of us is an evolving work of art, and this journal is designed to turn up the volume on that truth.

Are you ready to dive into your own life's adventure and cultivate your creative spirit? Are you willing to make your life a truly creative masterpiece?

Imagine transforming your life into a continuous discovery of body-mind-and-beyond magnificence. Engage in your own rich explorations through fun, mind-opening questions and activities that take your life from familiar to fantastic!

FIVE "SHAKE IT UP!" TOOLS FOR THE BEST RESULTS

Appreciation

In this journal, you are invited into self-appreciation as a way to fill your own cup with positive feelings. Appreciation can then spill over to those around you. By noticing something new, beautiful, and inherently good about yourself, you are more likely to notice the same things in others.

In case it's easier for you to start the appreciation with other people, please do so. Take the Appreciation Day suggestion and first apply it to somebody else and then try it on yourself.

Wonder Question

Wondering is a powerful whole-body tool to access the creative source within yourself and open up the flow of creative ideas. A Wonder Question is like tossing seeds out into the cosmos: it expresses free of any expectation of an immediate, specific answer. Think of wondering as a superpower that connects you to potentials beyond your familiar-thinking brain.

Wonder is spacious. When you ask a Wonder Question, let your rational mind expand and notice more space in your body and mind. In the grand realm of wonder, there is plenty of room for miracles to occur.

Shifting from Blame to Wonder

This is a powerful tool that consists of four elements: noticing that you are blaming or criticizing; accepting this fact; choosing to shift from blaming or criticizing; and creating a new experience for yourself.

Here is a step-by-step process for shifting from blame to wonder that you can use with each blame statement in the journal.

1. Have fun exaggerating your complaint.
2. Check to see if you are willing to shift from blame to wonder. This choice requires letting go of the grip of being "right." Choosing wonder shifts you out of the cycle of adrenaline and into the space of aliveness.
3. First, make the sound hmmm. Feel the vibration of the sound inside your body. There is scientific evidence that this sound unifies the two hemispheres of the brain.
4. Say the Wonder Question out loud a couple of times, each time adding the sound hmmm in front of it. You may change the question slightly to resonate with your own vocabulary.
5. Remember to add breath and movement. Notice if and how your body may want to move, and go ahead and move accordingly while saying the question.
6. Notice any changes in how you feel during and after asking the question.
7. As the day progresses, tune into your question(s) again and check to see how your body feels. In case any ideas or thoughts have surfaced, note these for yourself in some way.

Most importantly, add a dose or two of fun! Wonder is intended to be lighthearted and supportive of you feeling your best.

Creative Invitation

Put on your lab coat and get ready to experiment with new ways of interfacing with life as a discovery process.

The Creative Invitations in this journal are interactive, wholly experiential, and potentiallyeven FUN! Some invitations may seem very foreign and strange. Go for it anyway, even if just for the experiment of doing something strange. Simply allowing yourself to experiment with an open mind and heart creates friendly change from the inside out. Play within the explorations like you might try on a new fashion. The insights come after the experience and full participation is encouraged.

Verbing

Bring yourself into motion and generate a good time by tuning in and playing with a verb. We call this "verbing".

Active verbs are great for both your intellectual brain and your body brain. These verbs are about movement and movement is good medicine. Exploring active verbs invites the intellect, body intelligence, and new insights to weave together.

FIVE MASTER SKILLS TO PRACTICE
WITH EACH ACTIVITY

Move and breathe

Whether you are playing with a Wonder Question, Verbing, or Creative Invitation, please remember to move and breathe. Whenever possible, change the body posture, move in new ways, change your dominant hand, or create a dance. Notice your breathing. Is it relaxed, easeful, and pleasurable?

Notice your body sensations

Noticing your body sensations can help you to clarify your current experience. Your body is always communicating something. Research and careful observations show that, as a rule, we feel sadness across our high chest and upper throat, fear around the navel area, and anger in the jaw, back of neck, and across shoulders. Noticing your body sensations can open a whole new world of your body intelligence and relationship with your feelings.

Go for it! Express full out

When you play with an activity, give yourself permission to exaggerate your body posture and your movements. Play with the sound of your voice, emphasizing different words each time and trying various intonations and accents. If you choose to draw something, allow yourself to experiment with unexpected combinations of colors and shapes. Broaden the spectrum of your self-expression.

Let yourself be weird, open to having fun

There's a great joy to discover, accept, and play with the quirky, eccentric, goofy parts within! The journal welcomes your weirdness!

Love yourself at every turn

Love yourself for being willing to play, for wanting to learn and experience new things, for showing up as a courageous explorer, inventor, and innovator of your life. We love you for all of that!

WONDER AND BODY-MIND
ADVENTURES

Date___ / ___ / ___

Appreciation

Unique qualities I see and appreciate about me are ...
(e.g., kindness, easy-going nature, fiery passion, willingness to listen)

1. _____

2. _____

3. _____

4. _____

5. _____

Breathe and move with the following question:
Hmmm, I wonder ... How can I enhance and expand my unique abilities?

Write down any spontaneous thoughts, ideas, or actions that come to mind.

Date___ / ___ / ___

Creative Invitation

Today, turn your attention to what you have already accomplished.

Imagine yourself at the peak of a great hike. Turn back toward all the territory you have already covered, and give yourself permission to acknowledge what you have already completed and mastered (i.e., riding a bike, writing cursive, maintaining great friendships). Find the "wow" in the scenery of your life that you have already completed.

What would be a deeply satisfying way to acknowledge and express how you feel about your life so far?

Shift from Self-Blame to Wonder

Instead of thinking, "Nobody loves me"
Try: *Hmmm, I wonder ... How can I expand my ability to give and receive love?*

Exaggerate the blame statement until it seems kind of funny. Notice how your body shifts when you change from *blame to wonder.*

Write down what you notice: the changes in your body can be a clue for when you are in blame or in wonder.

Date____ / ____ / ____

Creative Invitation

Singing uses a different track in your nervous system from when you are simply talking. So, today, notice your inner voices, and sing them to yourself.

Write down at least three phrases that you regularly tell yourself (positive or negative) and sing them out loud to yourself.

How do you experience these phrases when you sing them?

Date___ / ___ / ___

Shift from Blaming the World to Wonder

Instead of thinking, "Life is so SCARY!"
Try: *Hmmm, I wonder ... How can I experience life as a friendly adventure?*

Describe the kind of adventure you are experiencing today.

Date___ / ___ / ___

Play with the Verb

Admire is to perceive with loving perspective, and see the beauty of who you are.

Begin by checking out some part of you that you already see as beautiful, and invite yourself to bask in admiration of yourself. BE MOVED by your own magnificent self.

What actions and body movements create an experience of admiration throughout your whole body?

Date___ / ___ / ___

Wonder Question

Hmmm, I wonder ... How can I enjoy spontaneous expressions?

Being spontaneous requires a bit of courage and willingness to act in the moment of inspiration with minimal thought.

Ask yourself:
Am I willing to allow myself to be spontaneous?
How can I let myself to be moved by my friendly impulses?

Date___ /___ /___

Appreciation

I appreciate how much I enjoy...
(e.g., writing, exercising, really great smells, combining colors)

1. _____

2. _____

3. _____

4. _____

5. _____

Breathe and move with the following question:
Hmmm, I wonder ... How can I give myself permission for even greater enjoyment?

Write down any spontaneous thoughts, ideas, or actions that come to mind.

Date___ / ___ / ___

Creative Invitation

Clearing the Pipes

Whining is NOT a crime. Whining is simply one way many people learned to express themselves in order to get the attention that is required when we're little.

Give yourself permission to whine full-out for 30 seconds using any whining phrase.
This one, for example: *YOU ALWAYS criticize me!*

Notice how giving yourself permission to "clear the pipes" affects your body and sense of your energy. Write down or draw what you notice.

What are your favorite whining phrases?
How can you express them with such enthusiasm that you begin to laugh?

Date___ / ___ / ___

Shift from Self-Blame to Wonder

Instead of thinking, "Something is obviously wrong with me"
Try: *Hmmm, I wonder ... How can I appreciate my unique differences?*

Write down the gifts embedded in those unique qualities you have judged as "wrong."

Date___ / ___ / ___

Creative Invitation

Vision cannot be realized without venture. Imagination rocks, yet without commitment and aligned action, what you imagine will likely stay in the realm of possibility rather than become reality.

Today, ask yourself, "What really turns me on?" Write it down here.

THEN, ask yourself, "What is one simple action step I can take to create this experience?"

Date___ / ___ / ___

Shift from Blaming the World to Wonder

Instead of thinking, "There's never enough money/love/time"
Try: *Hmmm, I wonder ... How can I generate and enjoy plenty of money/love/time?*
Or: *Hmmm, I wonder ... How can I experience myself as a source of money/love/time?*

What do you notice in your body when you ask yourself these Wonder Questions?

Date___ /___ /___

Play with the Verb

Adore is to look upon with utmost esteem, love and respect.

Designate a plush, warm blanket as your adoration blanket and wrap yourself up. What are you willing to adore about you right now?

How can you embrace yourself in your highest esteem?

Date___ / ___ / ___

Wonder Question

Hmmm, I wonder ... How can I experience my feelings as invitations for discovery?

Wisdom and creativity flow within the waves of your feelings. Let yourself draw a picture of your sadness, anger, fear, joy, or sexual feelings. What colors, textures, and images show up for you?

Date___ / ___ / ___

Appreciation

I see and appreciate my body, especially my...
(e.g. jiggly parts, butt, strong legs, round belly, blue eyes)

1. _____

2. _____

3. _____

4. _____

5. _____

Breathe and move with the following question:
Hmmm, I wonder ... How can I easily say yes to what nourishes my body?

Write down any spontaneous thoughts, ideas, or actions that come to mind.

Date____ / ____ / ____

Creative Invitation

The act of controlling is one way we each learned to create a sense of safety. Control is a whole body experience.

Cross your fingers, toes, arms, legs, and anything else you can think of as you try this to explore how to create a fully embodied experience of controlling.

Experiment with this statement: "Just control yourself, would you?"

Try to REALLY control yourself while saying this out loud, imagining to whom you would like to say this. As you repeat it a few more times, find new ways to control yourself. And then, in one instant, let go and go "out of control" with your body.

What images does "controlling yourself" bring up? And what image does "going out of control" bring up?

Date___ / ___ / ___

Shift from Self-Blame to Wonder

Instead of thinking, "How could I be so stupid?"
Try: *Hmmm, I wonder ... How can I cultivate and use my whole body intelligence make choices?*
(such as using my mind or my intuition, listening to the sensations in my body and feelings that arise).

Today, tune in to what movements can generate a connection through your whole body, especially as you are making decisions.

Date____ / ____ / ____

Creative Invitation

Often, one of the easiest ways to discover what is going on internally is to look around and notice what catches your attention externally.

For example, when you look outside, what do you see? And what lens do you look through? Do you see what is beautiful, peaceful, needs "fixing," etc.? How does what you see externally inform you about what you feel inside yourself?

In the space below, draw an inspiring landscape picture. (Perfection not required!)

After you complete your drawing, pause and take a breath or two. How can you invite this outer landscape picture to inspire how you see yourself?

Date___ / ___ / ___

Shift from Blaming the World to Wonder

Instead of thinking, "Life is so UNFAIR!"

Try: *Hmmm, I wonder … How can I extract wisdom from all of my experiences and embrace it?*

As you think about this Wonder Question, notice how your body sensations change. Write down any insights.

Play with the Verb

Amuse is to respond and give your attention in a light and enjoyable way.

What are your favorite ways to amuse yourself, to expand beyond the serious, and to be open to discovery? You are your own personal amusement park. What "ride" is your favorite?

Ask yourself: in any given situation, "How can I amuse myself and create a good time midst whatever is going on?"?

Date___ / ___ / ___

Wonder Question

Hmmm, I wonder ... How can I become masterful in focusing my attention by choice?

Today, notice how your body responds when you give something your attention by choice.

Date___ / ___ / ___

Appreciation

I appreciate several aspects of my whole body, such as...
(e.g. flexibility, strength, sensitivity, roundness, muscles)

1. _____

2. _____

3. _____

4. _____

5. _____

Breathe and move with the following question:
If my whole body could speak, what would it say?

Write down any spontaneous thoughts, ideas, or actions that come to mind.

Date___ /___ /___

Creative Invitation

When we contemplate a new idea or project, we often consider whether somebody will approve or disapprove our idea.

Take this phrase as an example: What will people think?

After asking this question out loud a few times, free your creative mind and let yourself begin to make up some really crazy, funny stories about what people might think about you. (Include reactions from totally impressed to utterly disgusted)

How do you allow these stories to impact how you feel about yourself?

Date___ / ___ / ___

Shift from Self-Blame to Wonder

Instead of thinking, "I'm just not creative"
Try: *Hmmm, I wonder ... How I can cultivate my unique creative expression?*

Look around and appreciate yourself for all the things in your life that you've already created.

Then think about this: What one choice will I make today that can take me into a new direction?

Creative Invitation

Right here, right now, describe what you are feeling inside as if you are making a weather report. (Foggy with a chance of rain, spotty clouds with strong sunshine, warm, etc.)

As you feel into your day, what's your inner weather prediction?

Date___ / ___ / ___

Shift from Blaming the World to Wonder

Instead of thinking, "Relationships are HARD!"
Try: *Hmmm, I wonder ... How can I invite ease into my relationships?*

What are three relationships that feel "hard"?
What feels "hard"?
How do you make it hard?
How can you invite ease?

Note down anything that comes to mind.

Date____ / ____ / ____

Play with the Verb

Caress is a soft and soothing energetic and/or physical touch that generates a sense of ease and communicates kindness.

What images emerge as you speak the word caress?
What voices might you use that vibrate the experience of being caressed?

How might you caress yourself with...fabric? Music? Food?

Date___ / ___ / ___

Wonder Question

Hmmm, I wonder ... How can I make friends with my old familiar fears?

What are some of your *familiar* fears?
How do these fears show up as a body experience?
How can you add breath to where you feel scared in your body?
What happens when you add breath?

Date___ / ___ / ___

Appreciation

Today, I appreciate that I see the world as...
(e.g., full of possibilities, colorful and majestic, friendly, offering new opportunities)

1. _____

2. _____

3. _____

4. _____

5. _____

Breathe and move with the following question:
Hmmm, I wonder … How can I see the world as a friendly place?

Write down any spontaneous thoughts, ideas or actions that arise.

Date___ / ___ / ___

Creative Invitation

Today, let yourself whine full-out.

Whine about whatever you wish. After a minute or so, drop the words out and let your sound and body movements express your displeasure.

With the intention to have some fun, see what happens when you let yourself stomp around while whining out loud. Make your biggest pouty lip EVER.

Notice what happens in your mind and your body when you go from serious to lighthearted. Write down anything you noticed.

Date____ / ____ / ____

Shift from Self-Blame to Wonder

Instead of thinking, "I'll never be good enough" OR "I am not good enough"

Try: *Hmmm, I wonder … What can I appreciate about me right now?*

Date___ / ___ / ___

Creative Invitation

A Health Tip Today:
One of the great predictors of good health is hanging around those people who really like you, and who you really like. Name at least 3 of those people here.

When you think about them, how do you notice your body responding?

Is there a new way you would like to express your caring and appreciation for them?

Shift from Blaming the World to Wonder

Instead of thinking, "People are so selfish"
Try: *Hmmm, I wonder … How can I practice and inspire generosity?*

What's one way you can choose to be generous today?

Pay attention also to any acts of generosity from other people today.

Date___ / ___ / ___

Play with the Verb

Celebrate is to express full sensory, wide, and wild appreciation.

What are you willing to celebrate about yourself right now?
What is your favorite way to celebrate?
What brand new way might you creatively celebrate yourself and others today?

Date___ / ___ / ___

Wonder Question

Hmmm, I wonder … How can I create easy connections with myself and others?

Today, notice what happens in your body when you connect with people.

What can you change about your breathing and body posture that will create ease for you when you are with others?

Date___ /___ /___

Appreciation

I appreciate how much I like to play with...
(e.g., words, humor, color, music, using my body, futuristic ideas)

1. _____

2. _____

3. _____

4. _____

5. _____

Breathe and move with the following question:
Hmmm, I wonder ... How can I expand the ways in which I play in the world?

Write down any spontaneous thoughts, ideas, or actions that come to mind.

Date___ / ___ / ___

Creative Invitation

Menu for Your Soul

It's not only our body that needs food, so does our soul.

Notice and jot down what nourishes you deeply, within and beyond your body. For example, nourishing yourself could be a brisk walk while listening to '60s songs.

Based on the depth of nourishment, put down items as different courses on the menu for your soul.

Hors d'oeuvre for My Soul:

Main Course for My Soul:

Dessert for My Soul:

Date____ / ____ / ____

Shift from Self-Blame to Wonder

Instead of thinking, "I'll never fit in"
Try the following Wonder Questions:
Hmmm, I wonder ... How can I be my own best company? OR
Hmmm, I wonder ... How can I enjoy my own company whether I am with people or alone?

What's great about being alone?
What do you really enjoy about your own company?
Write it down here.

Date___ / ___ / ___

Creative Invitation

Standing at the threshold of change, progress isn't always about launching forward.

Draw a circle on this page, which represents where you are right now. Now begin to feel and draw the "direction" and the quality of your progress for today.

How does this drawing inform you?
If it could speak, what would it tell you?
If you were to stand directly in the center of the "now" circle, what direction feels like the direction of progress?
Let your body respond.

Date___ /___ /___

Shift from Blaming the World to Wonder

Instead of thinking, "Stress is just a fact of life"
Try: *Hmmm, I wonder ... How can I shift into ease?*

In one column, write down three stressful things for you in this moment.
In a second column, write down, for each of the three things, the first step or a body movement that generates a felt sense of ease.

Date___ / ___ / ___

Play with the Verb

Cherish is to contact someone or something with tender care.

What or who is easy for you to cherish? Generate that tender feeling within yourself.
Now, imagine bathing yourself in it. How does the experience of cherishing change how you feel inside yourself?

Date___ / ___ / ___

Wonder Question

Hmmm, I wonder ... What does my body posture communicate to the world right now?

Discover the variety of your body postures and their special messages to the world.

Date___ /___ /___

Appreciation

I appreciate how much I have learned, especially in the area of...
(e.g., loving my body, how to listen, physiology, how to arrange flowers)

1. _____

2. _____

3. _____

4. _____

5. _____

Breathe and move with the following question:
Hmmm, I wonder ... How can I easily invest my attention in what I feel excited to learn?

Write down any spontaneous thoughts, ideas, or actions that come to mind.

Date___ / ___ / ___

Creative Invitation

Take a variety of selfies today. Make faces, try on and exaggerate the facial expressions of different emotions.

When you have a moment, go back and check out your selfies.

What's fun and lovable about each expression?

Date___ /___ /___

Shift from Self-Blame to Wonder

Instead of thinking, "I am such a failure"
Try: *Hmmm, I wonder … How I can see each outcome as an opportunity for discovery?*

Think of one perceived failure.

Then, shift your body posture, and ask, "What gifts and discoveries are being revealed from this experience?"

Date___ / ___ / ___

Creative Invitation

In nature, everything moves. Nothing stays the same.

Where in life have you been trying to keep something "the same"?
What do you imagine happening if you were to loosen your grip?
What is one friendly action step you can take to support movement
and change?

Date____ / ____ / ____

Shift from Blaming the World to Wonder

Instead of thinking, "People are not to be trusted"
Try: *Hmmm, I wonder … How can I source reliable agreements?*

How does your body respond to this Wonder Question?

Trust is an inside job, and comes with making and keeping reliable agreements.

Date ___ / ___ / ___

Play with the Verb

Choose is to actively select from a number of possibilities.

Give yourself permission to ask, "What do I really want?"

Dance with this question, literally, like with a dance partner. Breathe it in and let it circulate all the way through you.

What do YOU really want? Invite yourself to be "unreasonable" in your desires. Make a list of "what I really want."

How can you let yourself enjoy wanting?

Date___ / ___ / ___

Wonder Question

Hmmm, I wonder ... What creative ideas are hatching through me in this moment?

Date___ / ___ / ___

Appreciation

I appreciate how much I value...
(e.g., a clean house, my friendships, traveling, trying new foods)

1. _____

2. _____

3. _____

4. _____

5. _____

Date___ / ___ / ___

Creative Invitation

Creativity works best when the left brain and the right brain collaborate well together. The left brain loves structure. The right brain loves flow.

What types of structure support the flow of your creativity? It can be scheduling your creative time, or having a specific location that inspires you.

How can you invite your linear brain and your creative brain to make friends with each other?

Date___ /___ /___

Shift from Self-Blame to Wonder

Instead of thinking, "I am such a fraud"
Try: *Hmmm, I wonder … How can I love myself even when I question myself?*

What actions can I take to line up with the integrity of who I really am?

Date___ / ___ / ___

Creative Invitation

SMART IS BEAUTIFUL!

List all the ways in which you are really smart.

Date___ /___ /___

Shift from Blaming the World to Wonder

Instead of thinking, "THIS is REALLY serious!"
Try the following Wonder Questions:
Hmmm, I wonder ... How can I shift to experiencing and inspiring fun?
Hmmm, I wonder ... What can I find amusing about THIS?

Date___ / ___ / ___

Play with the Verb

Cultivate is to promote the growth of a new idea or pattern of living by investing your curious and positive attention.

Imagine yourself as your own garden.
What seeds have you planted or are you planting?
What is your familiar way of cultivating new ideas and experiences?
What is one new choice you can make to cultivate any new ideas?
What quality of attention would most serve your organic growth?

Date___ / ___ / ___

Wonder Question

Hmmm, I wonder ... Where is the humor in my current experience?

Date___ / ___ / ___

Appreciation

Several things I appreciate about my essential self are...
(e.g., my sense of humor, how I dress, that I am really smart, that I believe in magic)

1. _____

2. _____

3. _____

4. _____

5. _____

Breathe and move with the following question:
Hmmm, I wonder ... How can I create friendly opportunities to express myself?

Write down any spontaneous thoughts, ideas, or actions that come to mind.

Date___ / ___ / ___

Creative Invitation

Walk around all day strutting your stuff, saying to yourself (out loud or quietly): "I am a magnificent animal!"

Notice what happens to your posture and the way of moving when you invite in your magnificence.

Date___ / ___ / ___

Shift from Self-Blame to Wonder

Instead of thinking, "Something's really wrong about my body"
Try: *Hmmm, I wonder ... What am I willing to appreciate about my body now?*

Date___ /___ /___

Creative Invitation

Mastery requires a lot of practice, some say at least 10,000 hours.

What are you really wanting to master?
Where are you already masterful?

Write down the answers here, including one thing you can do to further your mastery in any subject.

Date___ / ___ / ___

Shift from Blaming the World to Wonder

Instead of thinking, "Everyone is just too darned busy"
Try the following Wonder Questions:
Hmmm, I wonder ... How can I create space to appreciate myself for all my skills?
Hmmm, I wonder ... How can I create time and space for what I love doing?

Date___ / ___ / ___

Play with the Verb

Delight is to give and invite great pleasure and enjoyment.

Close your eyes and breathe gently. When you open your eyes, allow yourself to be delighted in seeing something new, even in your familiar surroundings.

What do you notice?
Notice in your body, from where does your fountain of delight spring?
What are a few ways that you like to delight your physical senses?

Gift yourself those experiences just for the heck of it!

Date___ / ___ / ___

Wonder Question

Hmmm, I wonder ... What story can I make up about myself in favor of my greatness?

Rather than telling the story of any perceived shortcomings, what stories can you make up that highlight your magnificence?

Date___ / ___ / ___

Appreciation

I appreciate how easily I express my creativity through...
(e.g., my clothes, making music, organizing travel plans, photography, inspiring conversations)

1. _____

2. _____

3. _____

4. _____

5. _____

Breathe and move with the following question:
Hmmm, I wonder ... How can I expand my repertoire for expressing my creativity?

Write down any spontaneous thoughts, ideas, or actions that come to mind.

Date___ / ___ / ___

Creative Invitation

A Brain Dump

Give yourself one minute to say out loud everything you are thinking about. It does not matter if anything makes sense, just "dump" it all out.

Notice how your body and mind feel before and after the dump. You can also do this in writing.

Date___ /___ /___

Shift from Self-Blame to Wonder

Instead of thinking, "WHAT do you mean?! That's just the way I am"
Try: *Hmmm, I wonder ... What new aspects can I discover about myself?*

Date___ / ___ / ___

Creative Invitation

List below what's really working in your life.

Imagine what might happen if you focus your attention on what is working.

Date___ / ___ / ___

Shift from Blaming the World to Wonder

Instead of thinking, "Don't get too full of yourself!"
Try: Hmmm, I wonder … How can I fully (and outrageously) celebrate myself and others?

Date____ / ____ / ____

Play with the Verb

Discover is to realize fresh insight or wisdom about something previously unseen or unknown.

Choosing to live "in discovery" is a courageous choice and invites even familiar experiences to gain a sense of refreshment and adventure.

Choose something simple—a morsel of food, a flower, a leaf, the palm of your own hand, etc.—and check it out with "new" eyes. Begin to discover the nuances and precious uniqueness of what you are holding.

What is something new that you are discovering about yourself today?

.

Date___ / ___ / ___

Wonder Question

Hmmm, I wonder ... How can I enjoy being in direct contact with myself and others?

How do you like to be in contact with others?
How do you like to be contacted by others?

Date____ / ____ / ____

Appreciation

I really appreciate my intellect, especially my ...
(e.g., ability to remember important things, quick thinking, wide vocabulary, math skills)

1. _____

2. _____

3. _____

4. _____

5. _____

Breathe and move with the following question:
Hmmm, I wonder ... How can I enjoy all the ways in which I am really smart?

Write down any spontaneous thoughts, ideas, or actions that come to mind.

Date___ /___ /___

Creative Invitation

PLAY is an important aspect of our human development.

When you were a child, what did you most love to do? Write down a few of these activities. What did you really love about them?

Take a moment to consider: how does play show up in your life now? Moving forward, what activities can you engage in to grow a sense of play?

Date___ / ___ / ___

Shift from Self-Blame to Wonder

Instead of thinking, "Am I the only one who cares?"
Try: *Hmmm, I wonder ... How can I welcome genuine support?*

Date___ / ___ / ___

Creative Invitation

What's your current definition of beauty?

Let yourself use color, shapes, and your own beautiful words to describe
your definition of beauty.

Date___ /___ /___

Shift from Blaming the World to Wonder

Instead of thinking, "People never really change"
Try: *Hmmm, I wonder ... How can I see me and others fresh and new each day?*

Date___ / ___ / ___

Play with the Verb

Embrace is to invite and receive with warmth and welcoming.

When you embrace life, rather than arguing that you are having the "wrong" experience, you choose to accept an experience as it is.

Choose one pleasant experience, and ask yourself, as an "embrace": "What am I discovering through this experience?"
Now choose one not-as-pleasant experience, and ask yourself, as an "embrace": "What am I discovering through this experience?"

Date___ /___ /___

Wonder Question

Hmmm, I wonder ... What aspect of me is ripe and ready to blossom?

Date___ / ___ / ___

Appreciation

I appreciate the different ways in which I've stepped into the unknown, including ...
(e.g., testing new recipes, moving to a new place, connecting with a new friend, taking a new route home)

1.
_____

2.
_____

3.
_____

4.
_____

5.
_____

Breathe and move with the following question:
Hmmm, I wonder ... How can I cultivate friendly experiences with the unknown?

Write down any spontaneous thoughts, ideas, or actions that come to mind.

Date____ / ____ / ____

Creative Invitation

Create a playlist of 5 of your favorite songs.

Dance with each song and let all of them inspire new ideas. As ideas bubble up, jot them down here.

Date___ / ___ / ___

Shift from Self-Blame to Wonder

Instead of thinking, "What ELSE could happen to me?"
Try: *Hmmm, I wonder ... How I can source and invite friendly experiences into my life?*

Date___ / ___ / ___

Creative Invitation

Just as a seed is "destroyed" to allow the seedling to emerge, sometimes you've gotta be willing to let go of who you think you are in order to discover who you really are.

What opinions and beliefs about yourself are you now willing to grow beyond?

Date___ / ___ / ___

Shift from Blaming the World to Wonder

Instead of thinking, "What goes up must come down"
Try: *Hmmm, I wonder … How can I gently grow in my capacity for positive energy?*

Date____ / ____ / ____

Play with the Verb

Emerge is to come forth or arise into existence.

All people have had the experience of emerging: their own birth.

Ask yourself, "What's birthing through me now?"
Right now, how would you like to support this emergence?

Date___ / ___ / ___

Wonder Question

Hmmm, I wonder ... How can I experience my life as an invitation for discovery?

Date___ /___ /___

Appreciation

I appreciate all the ways I have contributed to ...
(e.g., designing my home, creating and maintaining great friendships, training my dog, inspiring honesty, caring for my family)

1. _____

2. _____

3. _____

4. _____

5. _____

Breathe and move with the following question:
Hmmm, I wonder ... What creative contributions are emerging through me now?

Write down any spontaneous thoughts, ideas, or actions that come to mind.

Date____ /____ /____

Creative Invitation

Choose three words that describe how you would like your day to feel. Write them down here.

Throughout the day, ask yourself how you can invite those qualities into whatever experience you are having.

Return here to write what you discovered.

Date____ / ____ / ____

Shift from Self-Blame to Wonder

Instead of thinking, "I sacrificed myself for him/her"
Try the following Wonder Questions:
Hmmm, I wonder ... How can I experience him/her as my ally? OR
Hmmm, I wonder ... How can we both have what we really want?

Date___ / ___ / ___

Creative Invitation

What happens inside you when you sit and do nothing?

Write or draw what you notice about your body after taking a few minutes to "do nothing."

Date___ / ___ / ___

Shift from Blaming the World to Wonder

Instead of thinking, "Love never lasts"
Try: *Hmmm, I wonder ... How can I see love as an endless field of discovery?*

Date___ / ___ / ___

Play with the Verb

Enchant is to conjure up and impart a magical quality to something, someone, or somewhere.

Imagine and create your personal magic wand, activating it with your own special spell.

How do you conduct magic through your body and through your wand?
What are your unique magical qualities and skills?

Date___ / ___ / ___

Wonder Question

Hmmm, I wonder … How can I invite my whole body to breathe?

Date ___ / ___ / ___

Appreciation

I appreciate the ways that my body supports me, especially ...
(e.g., telling me when I'm tired or hungry, during exercise, quick reaction time, muscular strength)

1. _____

2. _____

3. _____

4. _____

5. _____

Breathe and move with the following question:
Hmmm, I wonder ... How does my body like to be appreciated?

Write down any spontaneous thoughts, ideas, or actions that come to mind.

Date___ / ___ / ___

Creative Invitation

Take a few easy breaths, and let your curious attention scan your whole body with the sound hmmm...

As you breathe, say the following phrases out loud, repeating a few times if necessary, until you feel a sense of ease:

All of me is welcome here.
WOW!!
There's always plenty of love to go around.

Then make note of what happens with your body. Write down or draw what you notice.

Date___ / ___ / ___

Shift from Self-Blame to Wonder

Instead of thinking, "I clearly want too much"

Try: *Hmmm, I wonder ... How can I give myself permission to receive and appreciate all that I want?*

Date____ / ____ / ____

Creative Invitation

Dancing can be like laughing with your whole body. Play with dancing today in a way that feels amusing to your whole body.

Tune in and notice how your body responds. Write down what you notice.

Date____ / ____ / ____

Shift from Blaming the World to Wonder

Instead of thinking, "Why is the world/people so against me?"
Try: *Hmmm, I wonder ... How can I see the world/people as my allies?*

Date___ / ___ / ___

Play with the Verb

Enjoy is to literally be "in joy": to welcome and gather the benefits of pleasurable experiences.

Go ahead, get willing to raise your thermostat for joy and good times. There is no universal law that says we can only experience so much joy.

What "rules" have you made up that limit your joy?
Are you willing to question your "rules" and raise your thermostat?
What are a few things you would be willing to genuinely and deeply enjoy?
Now wonder … How can I expand my enjoyment of those things?

Date____ / ____ / ____

Wonder Question

Hmmm, I wonder ... What is my most alive choice at this moment?

Date___ / ___ / ___

Appreciation

A few things I appreciate about my relationship with feelings are ...
(e.g., how I notice what I am feeling, seeing my feelings as friends, how
deeply I feel things, how quickly they change)

1. _____

2. _____

3. _____

4. _____

5. _____

Breathe and move with the following question:
*Hmmm, I wonder ... How can I feel and express all of my feelings in satisfying
and friendly ways?*

Write down any spontaneous thoughts, ideas, or actions that come to
mind.

Date___ /___ /___

Creative Invitation

Today, walk around as if you ARE the person you wanted to be when you grew up. STRUT your stuff, and notice what happens.

How do you experience yourself?
How do you see others from this perspective?
How do you relate to the world from here?

Date___ / ___ / ___

Shift from Self-Blame to Wonder

Instead of thinking, "No one ever understands me"

Try the following Wonder Questions:

Hmmm, I wonder ... How can I communicate clearly?

Hmmm, I wonder ... How can I enjoy sharing my whole self whether or not others "get me"?

Hmmm, I wonder ... How can I communicate in easy, effective ways?

Date____ / ____ / ____

Creative Invitation

If you had a superpower, what would it be?
What superpower sounds the most fun to you?
What's your superpower?

Invite your body to respond, or just make up one superpower.

How does your superpower contribute to your happiness and to those around you?

Shift from Blaming the World to Wonder

Instead of thinking, "Money is the source of evil"
Try: *Hmmm, I wonder ... How I can create a friendly relationship with money?*

Date___ / ___ / ___

Play with the Verb

Enrich is to infuse with new kinds of energies such that everything feels richer.

What can you add right now that "makes richer" this moment?

Date___ / ___ / ___

Wonder Question

Hmmm, I wonder … What simple pleasures surround me in this moment?

Date___ / ___ / ___

Appreciation

Some things I often avoid appreciating in myself are ...
(e.g., my busy mind, when I get bossy, my sense of order, my judgments)

1. _____

2. _____

3. _____

4. _____

5. _____

Breathe and move with the following question:
Hmmm, I wonder ... How can I see all of me as lovable?

Write down any spontaneous thoughts, ideas, or actions that come to mind.

Date___ /___ /___

Creative Invitation

Today, take three connected breaths, invite your body to shift in posture and movement three times, then ask yourself: "What are three qualities of life that I'd like to experience today?" Write these down.

Then say them aloud to yourself and draw the shape and movement of these words.

How can these pictures influence your day today?

Date___ / ___ / ___

Shift from Self-Blame to Wonder

Instead of thinking, "Nobody really needs me"
Try the following Wonder Questions:
(Consider the possibility that nobody really needs you. Say it out loud using different voices and tones, emphasizing different words.)
Hmmm, I wonder ... How can I experience this possibility as a freedom?
Hmmm, I wonder ... How can I see myself and all others as fully capable and resource-full?

Date___ / ___ / ___

Creative Invitation

What if the universe is totally in favor of your success?

Write down one experience when it was easy to see how the universe was fully in favor of your success.

Write down one experience when you perceived that the universe was "against" you.
Ask, "How was this experience in support of my discovering something new about myself?"

Date___ / ___ / ___

Shift from Blaming the World to Wonder

Instead of thinking, "Success ruins people"

Try: *Hmmm, I wonder ... How can I welcome all the gifts of success?*

Date___ /___ /___

Play with the Verb

Experience is to personally encounter and feel through what is actually happening.

Your body is an amazing instrument through which you can experience life directly, through your sensations, body awareness, and intelligence.

Tune in right now ...

What body sensations are present?
Describe what you notice in color, shape, texture, quality of movement, and sound.

What body sensations easily get your attention?
Tune in ... if those sensations could speak, what are they wanting to communicate?

Date___ / ___ / ___

Wonder Question

Hmmm, I wonder ... How can I breathe to make space for whatever is happening?

Notice what happens when you breathe toward what is happening in your body. Describe here what you notice.

Date___ / ___ / ___

Appreciation

Today, I choose to appreciate aspects of myself that I have taken for granted, including ...
(e.g., my beautiful eyes, my singing voice, my love for privacy, my freedom)

1. _____

2. _____

3. _____

4. _____

5. _____

Breathe and move with the following question:
Hmmm, I wonder ... How can I fully engage with what comes easily to me?

Write down any spontaneous thoughts, ideas, or actions that come to mind.

Date____ /____ /____

Creative Invitation

What does freedom feel like in your body?

Say the word freedom aloud a few times, inviting your body to create a new sense of freedom.

Notice and write down the choices you could make today to feed your felt sense of freedom.

Date___ / ___ / ___

Shift from Self-Blame to Wonder

Instead of thinking, "Nothing I do matters"
Try: *Hmmm, I wonder ... How can I fully enjoy all my contributions?*

Date___ / ___ / ___

Creative Invitation

Everyone gets stuck.

With your whole body, take the posture/position that represents how you get stuck, in other words give yourself permission to embody 'stuck' ... REALLY STUCK!

Notice your thoughts. Write them down. How is being physically stuck familiar?

Now, make a few tiny movements in your body and invite them to ripple outward. Notice what happens.

Date___ / ___ / ___

Shift from Blaming the World to Wonder

Instead of thinking, "Real artists never make a good living"
Try: *Hmmm, I wonder ... How can I weave creativity and abundance?*

Date___ /___ /___

Play with the Verb

Explore is to set out and engage with life, with the intent for new discovery.

Claim yourself as a courageous explorer. Get willing to let go of familiar maps and charts and see the unknown as a friendly adventure.

Try on the energy of your favorite explorer (Indiana Jones, Lewis and Clark, Marco Polo, etc.). How do they stand, move and speak? How could this energy support a deeper exploration of yourself?

Explore new routes and paths to your favorite places, even letting your intuition guide you. What do you notice about your level of aliveness?

Date___ / ___ / ___

Wonder Question

Hmmm, I wonder ... What sound perfectly matches how I feel right now?

What is the sound of joy within me?
What is my sound of anger?
What is my current sound of fear?
What is my current sound of sadness?
How about of my sexual feelings?

Date___ / ___ / ___

Appreciation

In my home, I appreciate how I ...
(e.g., welcome others, clean up after myself, bring in fresh flowers)

1. _____

2. _____

3. _____

4. _____

5. _____

Breathe and move with the following question:
Hmmm, I wonder ... How can I create my home as a welcoming place?

Write down any spontaneous thoughts, ideas, or actions that come to mind.

Date____ / ____ / ____

Creative Invitation

Bring into your awareness someone you really admire. What qualities do they embody that you admire? Write these down.

Then let yourself dance around, imagining these qualities as your dance partner.

What are a few choices you could make today to embody these qualities yourself?

Date___ / ___ / ___

Shift from Self-Blame to Wonder

Instead of thinking, "I'll never get her/his/their approval"
Try the following Wonder Questions:
Hmmm, I wonder ... What do I really want?
Hmmm, I wonder ... How can I celebrate myself and my contributions?

Date___ / ___ / ___

Creative Invitation

Consider the question, "What in the world was I thinking?" or "What in the world were YOU thinking?"

Stand up straight and give yourself permission to wag your finger, pull at your hair, and shake your fists as you declare this question out loud. Start by using your own voice, and then invite yourself to get creative, expressing this using many different voices, including those that make you smile.

What do you notice as you begin to add your creativity to your declaration?

Date____ / ____ / ____

Shift from Blaming the World to Wonder

Instead of thinking, "Hard work is required for success"
Try: *Hmmm, I wonder … How can I create awesome success and abundance through ease?*

Date___ / ___ / ___

Play with the Verb

Express is to reveal my inner experiences through sound, movement, words, and creative means.

If experience is like an inhale, then expression is like an exhale. Inhaling and noticing, then exhaling and expressing what you notice. Expression doesn't always happen in words. It can also happen through sound, movement, art, music, etc.

How do you most like to express yourself?
What types of expression are most satisfying and life-giving to you?

Tune into one inner experience you are sensing right now. With your curious attention, grow that experience inside of you, then experiment with how those sensations want to express themselves. Play with sounds, movements, words, drawing, emotion, etc.

How can you create plenty of time and space to fully express?

Date___ / ___ / ___

Wonder Question

Hmmm, I wonder ... How can I expand myself to genuinely enjoy the unknown?

Date___ / ___ / ___

Appreciation

I appreciate how I listen to my body and follow my impulses to ...
(e.g., go to the bathroom, connect with others, know what I want to
eat, change my body posture)

1. _____

2. _____

3. _____

4. _____

5. _____

Breathe and move with the following question:
Hmmm, I wonder ... What is my body communicating with me right this moment?

Write down any spontaneous thoughts, ideas, or actions that come to
mind.

Date____ / ____ / ____

Creative Invitation

What lights you up?
What enlivens you and makes you smile?
Name one way that you can include this in your world today—and do it.

How does this choice influence your day?

Date___ / ___ / ___

Shift from Self-Blame to Wonder

Instead of thinking, "I'm such a mess!"
Try the following Wonder Questions:
Hmmm, I wonder ... How can I embrace all of me?
Hmmm, I wonder ... How can I welcome all of me, even the messy bits?

Date____ /____ /____

Creative Invitation

Imagine fully plugging into the space of infinite possibility.
Create your own unique image of firm, strong connection with this space.

What's your current relationship with infinite possibility?
How would like your relationship with infinite possibility to be?
How does your body feel when you give yourself permission to plug in all the way?

Date___ / ___ / ___

Shift from Blaming the World to Wonder

Instead of thinking, "It's just the way things are done!"
Try: *Hmmm, I wonder ... How can I open myself to new creative solutions?*

Date___ /___ /___

Play with the Verb

Harmonize is to attune myself to what is happening in ways that widen and enrich the current melody of life.

Harmonizing is not just about music. It can also be about harmonizing with animals, experiences, situations, nature and people. Harmonizing is a choice to be attuned with something or someone, honoring the "melody" of what is already happening and then weaving in your unique contributions.

How do you most like to blend yourself with others?
How do you most like to be harmonized with?

In a conversation, pause for a moment to feel its "tune," then ask yourself: "How can I harmonize with the melody of this conversation or experience?

Date___ / ___ / ___

Wonder Question

Hmmm, I wonder ... How can I easily focus my energy on what I love?

134

Date___ / ___ / ___

Appreciation

Several things that I appreciate about my breathing are …
(e.g., how I notice my breathing, how deep belly breathing energizes me, that my sinuses are clear)

1. _____

2. _____

3. _____

4. _____

5. _____

Breathe and move with the following question:
Hmmm, I wonder … How can all parts of my body breathe?

Write down any spontaneous thoughts, ideas, or actions that come to mind.

Date___ /___ /___

Creative Invitation

In the space below, draw a symbol of how you felt as a kid. Then draw a symbol of who you wanted to be when you grew up.

Are you willing to be or become the person you wanted to be?

Draw a variety of ways to connect these symbols, and play with being both child and adult. What insights arise from this?

Date____ / ____ / ____

Shift from Self-Blame to Wonder

Instead of thinking, "I don't have a minute for myself!"
Try the following Wonder Questions:
Hmmm, I wonder ... How can I enjoy plenty of time?
Hmmm, I wonder ... How can I enjoy being with myself and all my feelings?

Date____ / ____ / ____

Play with the Verb

Reflect is to bring back an image, expression, or experience into yourself such that it offers an opportunity for inquiry and discovery.

When you look in a mirror, where do you put your attention? All you see is a reflection of who you are and an opportunity to own and expand your lovability.

Take a few minutes to ponder your life's greatest moments.
What qualities did those experiences reflect about you?
What are life's reflections inviting you to see and love now?

Date___ / ___ / ___

Shift from Blaming the World to Wonder

Instead of thinking, "Who am I to take on the world?"
Try: *Hmmm, I wonder ... How can I effectively express my creative power?*

Date___ / ___ / ___

Play with the Verb

Indulge is to be lavish in fulfilling your soul's deepest desires.

Indulging yourself is an opportunity to increase your capacity for positive life experiences. One at a time, choose something in which to indulge each of your senses separately for at least a full minute.

Touch
Taste
Smell
Sound
Movement
Sight
Imagination

How can you allow these indulgences to increase your capacity to enjoy life even more?

Date___ / ___ / ___

Wonder Question

Hmmm, I wonder ... What already feels great about me?

How can I vibrate this experience throughout my whole self?

Date____ / ____ / ____

Appreciation

I appreciate my sensory systems for noticing ...
(e.g., beautiful clothes, the warmth of sunshine on my skin, the good quality of sound, the nuances of taste)

1. _____

2. _____

3. _____

4. _____

5. _____

Breathe and move with the following question:
Hmmm, I wonder ... What most delights each of my senses?

Write down any spontaneous thoughts, ideas, or actions that come to mind.

Creative Invitation

Call up Your Inner Poet

Here are a few poem starters as a warm up. Let your inner poet write a line or two in response. If you get stuck, write with your non-dominant hand.

It's time to ...
The magic flowed from ...
While the trees waved their long branches ...
The dreamer dreams visions of ...
Suddenly, I broke out into song and ...

Date___ / ___ / ___

Shift from Self-Blame to Wonder

Instead of thinking, "I'll never get over 'THIS' ..."
"I thought I was already over THIS"
Try these Wonder Questions:
Hmmm, I wonder ... How can I see my life as an ongoing adventure of discovery?
Hmmm, I wonder ... How can I embrace all of my life as an ongoing adventure?

Date___ / ___ / ___

Play with the Verb

Inquire is to seek and discover by asking really good questions.

Really good questions and curiosity are far more powerful than knowing defined answers. Really good questions are an invitation for new possibilities and living into life's responses to these questions.

What are three really juicy questions you would be willing to inquire into, and invite your life to become the response? (e.g., How can I gloriously thrive in my life by simply being who I am?)

Date___ / ___ / ___

Shift from Blaming the World to Wonder

Instead of thinking, "WE are all doomed"

Try these Wonder Questions:

Hmmm, I wonder ... If I were to draw, dance, and/or make the sounds of 'doomed', what would it look or sound like?

Hmmm, I wonder ... What can I do today to produce positive, measurable results?

Date___ / ___ / ___

Play with the Verb

Savor is to receive and linger in the full sensory enjoyment of any experience.

Savoring is often the result of giving yourself ample timing to really enjoy something, be it a food, experience, place, person, or scent. Savoring is the art of whole-body enjoyment.

When was the last time you genuinely savored something? What was it? Describe how you experienced it in detail. SAVOR the experience now.

Find something to savor in your current experience. What happens when you allow plenty of time to absorb your full enjoyment?

Date___ / ___ / ___

Wonder Question

Hmmm, I wonder ... What areas of my body love to laugh?

Date____ / ____ / ____

Appreciation

I appreciate how I source my own ...
(e.g., good times, healthy choices, authority and approval, sense of lovability)

1. _____

2. _____

3. _____

4. _____

5. _____

Breathe and move with the following question:
Hmmm, I wonder ... How can I experience myself as the source of my well-being?

Write down any spontaneous thoughts, ideas, or actions that come to mind.

Date___ / ___ / ___

Creative Invitation

What random acts of kindness feel inspiring for you today? List three to five acts.

Write these down and begin to imagine how/when/with whom you might fulfill these actions.

Return here later and jot down how each influenced your own inner experience.

Shift from Self-Blame to Wonder

Instead of thinking, "I'm TRYING my hardest!"
Try these Wonder Questions:
Hmmm, I wonder ... What are the gifts that come from trying really hard?
Hmmm, I wonder ... How can I open myself to ease and play?

What happens when you open yourself to ease?
Does your productivity increase or decrease?
What structures support your productivity and creativity?

Play with the Verb

Smile is an easy, opening sensation of joy through your whole body.

Pretty much everyone knows how to smile with the mouth. Try on a full-out toothy grin, a "knowing" smile, a "come hither" smile, and even a gentle smile you would give a new friend. Notice what feels most natural and easy for you.

If different areas of your body could smile, how might that look and feel?
How can you smile with your eyes?
How can you smile from your heart?
How might your belly smile? How about your knees? And your toes?
How can you allow joy to be expressed through your whole body?

Shift from Blaming the World to Wonder

Instead of thinking, "Money doesn't grow on trees"
Try: *Hmmm, I wonder … How can I generate financial abundance with ease?*

Date____ / ____ / ____

Play with the Verb

Notice is to give pure attention and perceive.

The word notice comes from the root of a word that means "to be known or seen."

How can you give attention to yourself with a feather-light quality, and simply "notice" what is here?
When you give yourself pure attention, what do you notice? What body sensations draw your notice?
When you give yourself critical attention, what do you notice?
When you give yourself appreciative attention, what do you notice?
What wants to be appreciated within you right now?

Date___ / ___ / ___

Wonder Question

Hmmm, I wonder ... What am I willing to risk and include in support of my aliveness?

Date___ / ___ / ___

Appreciation

I appreciate how I gracefully connect with ...
(e.g., my beauty, relatives across the world, what I really want, new people)

1. _____

2. _____

3. _____

4. _____

5. _____

Breathe and move with the following question:
Hmmm, I wonder ... How can I enhance and enrich all of my connections?

Write down any spontaneous thoughts, ideas, or actions that come to mind.

Date____ / ____ / ____

Creative Invitation

Take a few moments and turn your body in the direction of your past.

As you peer over your past, in what ways have you already expressed courage? Creativity? Kindness?

Write these down, and notice what happens when you allow yourself to acknowledge them.

Date___ / ___ / ___

Shift from Self-Blame to Wonder

Instead of thinking, "I'm always one step behind everyone else."
Try the following Wonder Questions:

Hmmm, I wonder ... How can I learn what I most want to learn by observing the experiences of others, as well as through my own experiences?"

Hmmm, I wonder ... How I can embrace myself as whole and complete right this moment?

Date___ /___ /___

Play with the Verb

Nourish is to encourage growth by infusing generous genuine care.

Nourishment means so much more than feeding ourselves. Nourishment is absorbed from the inside-out and the outside-in, often all at the same time.

Ask yourself, "What truly nourishes me?"
Foods
Music
People
Places
Animals
Scents
Movements

Are you willing to give yourself what nourishes you? How can you choose that right now?

Shift from Blaming the World to Wonder

Instead of thinking, "Technology SUCKS!"
Try the following Wonder Questions:
Hmmm, I wonder ... How can I see technology as my ally in creating what I want?
Hmmm, I wonder ... How can I use technology to create meaningful connections?

Date___ / ___ / ___

Play with the Verb

Source is to claim yourself as the origin/well-spring from which your experiences begin.

Try these statements on:
"I source my joy."
"I source my safety."
"I source my own love."
"I am the source of my feelings."
"I am the source of my money."
"I am the source of my time."

Notice what happens.
What sensations come with claiming responsibility for your life experiences?

Date___ / ___ / ___

Wonder Question

Hmmm, I wonder ... How can I choose to participate fully in THIS moment?

Date___ /___ /___

Appreciation

I appreciate how I reliably complete ...
(e.g., my laundry, projects, communications, relationships that don't work)

1. _____

2. _____

3. _____

4. _____

5. _____

Breathe and move with the following question:
Hmm, I wonder ... What is ready to be completed in my life?

Write down any spontaneous thoughts, ideas, or actions that come to mind.

Date___ /___ /___

Creative Invitation

What are three things that feel as if they weigh you down?
Where in your body do you experience the weightiness?
How does your body want to move to make space around the "weightiness"?

What are three things that uplift you?
Using your body, express how you feel their uplifting power?
In what easeful ways can you connect to this power?

Shift from Self-Blame to Wonder

Instead of thinking, "I can't stand it anymore!"
Try: *Hmmm, I wonder ... How can I get clear and create what I really want?*

Play with the Verb

Nurture is to foster, support, and encourage growth.

True nurturance comes both from within and through our outside choices and inner experiences.

What are ways that you love to be nurtured?
How can you nurture all of your physical senses and desires?
How can you open to allow yourself to be nurtured by others?

Date___ /___ /___

Shift from Blaming the World to Wonder

Instead of thinking, "The world is a dangerous place"
Try: *Hmmm, I wonder ... How can I see the world as a friendly ally?*

Date___ / ___ / ___

Play with the Verb

Thrive is to prosper and grow vigorously.

Thriving is the experience that is possible beyond the boundaries of simple survival.
What choices could you make that move you beyond survival to thriving?

Date___ /___ /___

Wonder Question

Hmmm, I wonder ... How can I make appreciation my foundation for all my relationships and interactions?

Date___ / ___ / ___

Appreciation

I appreciate how I challenge myself to ...
(e.g., discover new things, exercise, take responsibility, let go of old stuff)

1. _____

2. _____

3. _____

4. _____

5. _____

Breathe and move with the following question:
Hmmm, I wonder ... How can I challenge myself in friendly ways?

Write down any spontaneous thoughts, ideas, or actions that come to mind.

Date___ /___ /___

Creative Invitation

What is one really fat, juicy, unreasonable question that you'd be willing to ask today?
How does the act of asking the question shifts your inner sense of yourself?

Date___ / ___ / ___

Shift from Self-Blame to Wonder

Instead of thinking, "Why is this happening to me?"
Try: *Hmmm, I wonder ... How is this experience contributing to my wholeness?*

Date___ / ___ / ___

Play with the Verb

Pamper is to treat with extreme kindness and care.

What does the notion of being fully pampered bring up for you?
What activities or actions do you include in your definition of pampering?
What acts of extreme kindness are you willing to gift to yourself today?

Date___ / ___ / ___

Shift from Blaming the World to Wonder

Instead of thinking, "Dreams are for fools"
Try: *Hmmm, I wonder ... How can I enjoy dreaming up a new reality?*

What are your dreams for the universe, for the world, for the people you love, and for yourself?

Play with the Verb

Venture is to embark upon a journey into the unknown.

Venturing is about going on a journey, whether inwardly or outwardly, and your movement can be large and in leaps, or in baby steps.

How do you prefer to venture into the unknown?
How can you make your venture as exciting as your arrivals?

Date ___ / ___ / ___

☀?☀

Wonder Question

Hmmm, I wonder ... What aspect of me or my body is calling for loving attention?

Date___ / ___ / ___

Appreciation

I appreciate the ordinary things in my life, including ...
(e.g., the warmth of my house, a beautiful tea cup, the sound of the crickets outside, having clean water)

1. _____

2. _____

3. _____

4. _____

5. _____

Breathe and move with the following question:
Hmmm, I wonder ... What simple pleasures surround me in this moment?

Write down any spontaneous thoughts, ideas, or actions that come to mind.

Date___ / ___ / ___

Creative Invitation

Every hour or so throughout the day, say to yourself (out loud, in the mirror, whispering, singing, etc.):
"Who I am is enough," and/or
"Who I am is plenty."

After a whole day of reminding yourself of this, notice how you feel. Record it here.

Date___ / ___ / ___

Shift from Self-Blame to Wonder

Instead of thinking, "Why do I always get the dirty work?"
Try: *Hmmm, I wonder ... How can I consistently choose what I really want?*

Date___ /___ /___

Play with the Verb

Receive is to accept an offering, be it the gifts of wisdom, gifts, love, or feedback.

Receiving is an active process. In the act of receiving, you make yourself available to accept what is being offered to you.

How would you describe your relationship to receiving (e.g., awkward, passive, enthusiastic)?
How do you know when you are open to receiving?
What is your experience when someone fully receives something you offer?
How might you stretch and flex your receiving muscles?

Date___ / ___ / ___

Shift from Blaming the World to Wonder

Instead of thinking, "Life's a bitch and then you die"
Try these Wonder Questions:
Hmmm, I wonder ... What can I appreciate about this very moment?
Hmmm, I wonder ... What can I appreciate about today?

Date___ / ___ / ___

Wonder Question

Hmmm, I wonder ... What am I willing to be grateful for right now?

Date____ /____ /____

Play with the Verb

Welcome is to meet a person or experience with warmth and kindness.

Let the word "welcome" roll around in your mouth a few times.

What aspects and expressions of you are you willing to welcome now?
Draw a picture below of your ideal image of welcoming.
How can you give this to your whole self?

POWERFUL OUTCOMES

These journal explorations have powerful outcomes. On the next few pages, invite yourself to check in and notice your realizations that have arisen from your participation with these activities.

REALLY HAPPY SURPRISES

... expressing moments of synchronicity and magic

SPONTANEOUS INSIGHTS

... random bursts of wisdom and guidance

REFLECTION COLLECTION

… positive things that people are saying about me

CELEBRATIONS AND NEXT STEPS!

Congratulations!

You jumped in, played, and discovered!!! This alone is no small feat, since it takes a courageous heart to explore new territories and possibilities.

Now it's time to take a few breaths, turn back toward the terrain you covered, and appreciate yourself and the view.

Invest plenty of time in your review, and all the ways in which you've grown in the process. To be "in process" is enough. In fact, "in process" means you are participating with life and all its riches.

If you feel inspired, start at the beginning again. Odds have it that you will create an entirely new experience the second time round, since your "starting line" is who and where you are now, after having explored the journal once.

Most of all, know yourself as an explorer, a life scientist, and a creator. The skills you've refined in these past months can serve you every day. Ask questions. Appreciate yourself. Make new choices. Explore new territories.

SHAKE IT UP by choice. You're worth it!

STAY CONNECTED

Please share the journal with your friends and loved ones and stay connected. Like *The Shake It Up! Journal* Facebook page.

Audrey Hazekamp is a Master coach and the founder of Tall Poppy Inc., standing for full engagement living…applying questions and practical actions that shake up the status quo and move potentials into realities. Her passion for high octane living is awe inspiring. Audrey's current home-base is Santa Barbara, California.
www.tallpoppyinc.com

Oxana Holtmann is a life coach and an advisor to international families and globally mobile professionals. She is the founder of Oxana Holtmann International, a coaching platform that promotes true homecoming through mindfulness, body intelligence, wonder and co-creativity at work and in relationships. Oxana loves writing, discovering and sharing practical wisdom, and noticing everyday beauty. Oxana grew up in Siberia and now lives with her family in Washington, D.C.
www.oxanaholtmann.com

SPECIAL THANK YOU!

We are grateful to Caitlin Powell for the journal's beautiful cover design! www.beckonhouse.com

Front cover image is brought into color by Audrey Hazekamp and designed by a talented artist Joni MacCracken in her book Color Your Essence - a coloring book for the creative in you.
www.jonimaccracken.com